C000148178

Published by Ice House Books

Thunderbirds™ and © ITC Entertainment Group Limited 1964, 1999 and 2019.
Licensed by ITV Ventures Limited. All rights reserved.

Compiled and edited by Samantha Rigby
Designed by Rhys Kitson

Ice House Books is an imprint of Half Moon Bay Limited
The Ice House, 124 Walcot Street, Bath, BA1 5BG
www.halfmoonbay.co.uk

All rights reserved. No part of this book may be reproduced, stored in
a retrieval system, communicated or transmitted in any form or by any
means without prior written permission from the publisher.

The material in this publication is of the nature of general comment only, and does not
represent professional advice. To the maximum extent permitted by law, the author and
publisher disclaim all responsibility and liability to any person, arising directly or indirectly
from any person taking or not taking action based on the information in this publication.

ISBN 978-1-912867-04-2

Printed in China

CLASSIC HERO
Handbook

ICE HOUSE BOOKS

Get your TEAM behind you

"OK, boys. That's the brief. It's our first assignment, so make it good."
– *Jeff Tracy*

Be ready to

jump into
ACTION
at any moment

"We're not just going to sit back and do nothing!"
– Scott Tracy

MAINTAIN ORDER *through* DISCIPLINE

"All right, Gordon, you're next. You go to your room.
Either you or Virgil has eaten the transmitter."
– *Jeff Tracy*

Accept

that you won't

ALWAYS
BE RIGHT

"Bedtime at home, breakfast-time in Monte Bianco.
Sometimes, even I get confused!"
– *Brains*

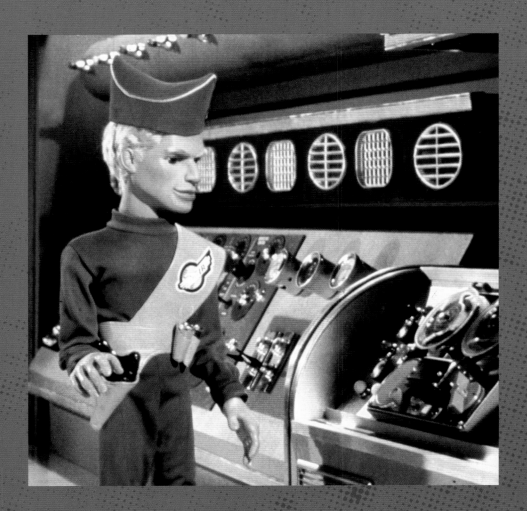

PLACE YOUR team members where they will best serve the TEAM

"Sure gets lonely up here. It's so quiet."
– John Tracy

ALWAYS ASK, *never assume*

"Where to, M'lady?"
– Parker

If you say things
FIRMLY ENOUGH,
people will think you know
WHAT YOU'RE DOING

"Right. You know the plan. Get to your positions."
– *Scott Tracy*

INTERNATIONAL RESCUE

RESPECT

YOUR TOOLS

"I am beside myself with admiration. It is the most vicious weapon I have ever seen!"
– *The Hood*

Understand

YOUR STRENGTHS AND DELEGATE

where appropriate

"I'm putting Tin-Tin and Scott in charge of the shopping arrangements this year."
– *Jeff Tracy*

MAKE SURE YOUR TEAM stay ready

"We can't ignore the possibility of another attack..."
– *Jeff Tracy*

MORE OFTEN THAN NOT,

a pre-mission

drink

IS NECESSARY

"Sorry to keep you waiting, M'lady."
– Parker

SOMETIMES A FEELING

is as good

as a solid plan

"What I'm gonna ask you to do will sound crazy,
but I have a hunch it'll work...."
– *Brains*

MAKE SURE YOU PICK A

GOOD

FROM WHICH
TO WATCH THE

CHAIR

ACTION

"Well, Tin-Tin, another rescue is under way."
– *Jeff Tracy*

HONESTY
is the best policy

Virgil Tracy: Was he as handsome as me, Gordon?

Gordon Tracy: Nearly Virgil, nearly.

When you're losing,

use any tactics necessary to

STOP

your opposition in their tracks

"I'm gonna get the restraining outfit."
– *Scott Tracy*

Kick back _sometimes_

AND LET THE KIDS DO THE WORK

"I guess you're right, Penny. Scott must run the show
on his own without any interference from me."
— _Jeff Tracy_

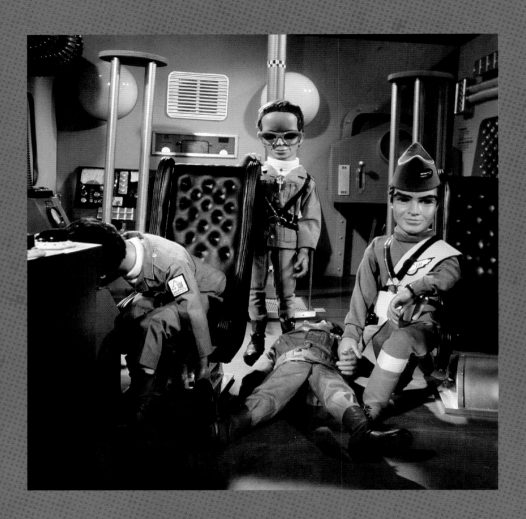

KEEP THE WELFARE OF OTHERS IN MIND

"The two boys don't look too good, Scott. The sooner we get them out of here the better, I should say."
– *Brains*

Confuse the ENEMY

the

WITH YOUR SMOULDERING

good looks

"Come on. Come and get me."
– *Alan Tracy*

Be honest about the CHALLENGES your team are facing

"There are only seven hours before the rocket blasts off."
– *John Tracy*

You can always find a **GOOD** reason to take a **BACK SEAT**

"Well, I don't like to pester the boys with needless radio calls when they're in the midst of a rescue."

– *Jeff Tracy*

Remember that occasionally

PEOPLE

will mess you around

"Pack the cases, unpack the cases. You'd think
some people would make up their minds."
— Parker

Sometimes RUNNING AWAY is the answer

"Leaving earth's atmosphere in 10 seconds."
– Alan Tracy

Make sure

EVERYBODY
UNDERSTANDS

your importance

"Not so involved? Let me tell you ... when this baby blasts
out into space, I'm the one that's in charge!"
– *Alan Tracy*

DIG DEEP
and find something
POSITIVE
to say after every
MISSION

"Well, boys, I guess you all did a swell job."
– Jeff Tracy

Prepare **amazing**

FACTS to make you look

intelligent

"I've been studying Manhattan Island, Mr Tracy. Its base is solid rock."
– *Brains*

Always have a pep talk ready

"Right, fellas, it's International Rescue all systems go! Good luck!"
– Scott Tracy

Take a moment each day to reflect on how

wonderful

YOU ARE

"The things I do for International Rescue..."
– *Scott Tracy*

Delegating can be
HARD WORK,
BUT YOU KNOW WHEN YOU'VE
done it right

"I've got a feeling about this one."
– *Jeff Tracy*